The Harborside Inn

A HISTORY FROM 1914 TO 1980

THE HARBORSIDE   EDGARTOWN, MASS.

LEO P. CONVERY

To order additional copies of this book, contact:
Xlibris
844-714-8691
www.Xlibris.com
Orders@Xlibris.com

ISBN: Softcover   978-1-6698-7250-4
        EBook   978-1-6698-7251-1

Print information available on the last page

Rev. date: 04/12/2023

Harborside Inn   1922

Preface

The Harborside Inn is located on South Water St. The original main building dates back to the early 17 hundreds. When it was being modified in the early 30's British coins were found when a wall was opened up. Most likely from the British occupation in 1812. The land beneath the Inn extends all the way down to Edgartown Harbor and is the only Island Inn to enjoy direct waterfront. The Inn is located right in the central part of the town, steps from the main four corners.

Edgartown was originally a small fishing village, and gained some notoriety during the whaling era when wealthy Captains built the rows of large homes in the town. It is now a home to very wealthy summer residents. Edgartown is one of 5 towns on the Island of Martha's' Vineyard and is located about 20 miles off the south coast of Cape Cod. Access is by Ferry from Woods Hole Mass, air from Boston or New York City, and private plane or boat.

The main building of the Inn was purchased by Tony Prada in 1914, taken over by his son in law Leo J. Convery and daughter Irene Louise Prada in 1930 after his untimely death. Over the next 48 years, Leo and Irene Convery would turn the Inn into a prime destination resort.

This story is being told by their only son, Leo P. Convery as recollected by him growing up on the island in the Inn and real Estate business. I am now within months from my 90th birthday, and this will allow me to exercise my memory pods as I try to relive and record this history and the incredible exploits of my parents and the hotel they built. March 2023

A History of the Harborside Inn, the Convery and Prada family's operations

The history of the Inn to be covered in this book will cover from 1900, up until 1978. The senior Converys started as a couple from 1930. It is a record of this couple's performance over a lifetime to create one of the best and most and most successful businesses on Martha's Vineyard. All told from the perspective of the son's memories and ramblings of his time growing up as the innkeeper's son.

1900 to 1929

The people who made it happen.

The Inn was started by children of immigrants, first year citizens of United States.

The patriarch on the Island side was from the Azores, Antone Enos Prada, born in 1842 in St. George. He married Isabel Augusta Sylva, in Edgartown. Isabelle was born in 1856 in St George. They had 8 children Frank, John, Antone Jr., Manuel, Louise, Joe, Mary, and Ernest. Antone Sr. started a farm in Edgartown which is at the head of the Cleveland town Road as it meets Road to the plains, now owned by Sally Brewster.

Antone Prada Jr. Was born in Oak Bluffs, in 1881, he lived in Edgartown, and was listed in several Census as a fisherman to yacht captain. He met Jane Hoey of New Bedford, and they married in 1902. Jane or Jenny as she was called was born in Glasgow in 1880. They had one daughter, Irene Louise Prada. Born in 1905 in Oak Bluffs at the Marthas Vineyard Hospital.

Irene will marry Leo J. Convery of Worcester, Mass. He is the son of Leo Constantine Convery Sr. from County Armah, Ireland, and Marjorie Labrie of France. He grew up in Worcester, Mass. Irene Louise Prada will marry Leo John Convery in Edgartown in 1929.

Antone Jr. (Tony) will purchase what will become the Inn, which was then a rooming house, with one main building on South Water Street in 1914. He will use this as a home and rooming house. The main structure of the Inn is estimated to date back to the 1700's. This will be the central piece of the developing Inn. Tony goes on to accumulate 3 other parcels between this property and Main Street, and by 1922 has acquired all the land between Osborn's Wharf and the corner piece owned by Chester Pease on Main and South Water St.

A key parcel is the Bird Property on the harbor by Osborn's wharf. This parcel includes the old Edgartown Yacht Club's building at the foot of Main St. In 1922, when the Club moves into a new facility at the end of Osbornes Wharf, Tony buys it. He converts the Yacht Club building to a home. This is the site of the Captain Prada House now. The lower portion of the property will become the home of the "Boathouse Bar" in the 1940's, the "Navigator Restaurant" in the 60's and The "Atlantic" restaurant and Club in 2004. But before all that happens, Tony builds a small rental cottage on the land with a large part overhanging into the harbor on pilings into water.

Tony will go on to make some big changes to the Inn, doubling the part facing the harbor, adding 4 rooms on the top floor, a first floor (street Level) dining room. And two rooms on the garden level. The kitchen will still be in the cellar under the main part of the building.

Harborside Inn Garden, Edgartown, Mass. on the Island of Martha's Vineyard.

Antone Prada 1925

Jane Prada 1922

1920

1920 Tony Prada

Antone E, Prada
Isabele L. Prada
Louise & Mary

Antone Enos Prada Sr.

Isabele L. Prada,

Daughters

Mary & Louise..

Irene Prada 1925

Irene at Northfield school

The early photos of the Inn show a gable addition facing the water with one window under the roof gable and then' a 1927 photo shows this has been doubled in size with 4 windows under the roof and six windows across on the lower mid-section.

The Edgartown waterfront in the 1900 to the 1940's was basically a working waterfront. Commercial fishing is big business and offshore draggers, and commercial boats are very much visible. Cat boats rigged for fishing and long trips are tied to stakes in the harbor in front of the Inn. In this period, they are very active in commercial fishing. Some captains took their vessels all the way to the Chesapeake to follow schools of Mackerel up the coast.

A walk along Dock Street at that time and up to 40's would reveal a commercial working harbor. Dock Street is the street that goes along the harbor. Starting at the end of Main Street is the Osbornes wharf and Sam Osbornes gas station, serving cars and Boats. Rows of fisherman huts, line the forward part along the harbor. These are used to store gear, or to clean fish, and open Shellfish in season. The new Edgartown Yacht Club and a Fish Market stand at the end of Osborne's Wharf where Whaling ships were based not so long ago. On the land side of Dock St. is a Welder with coal fired hearth. The gear and metal he uses for his work lines the street front entrance to the shop. Next come two large commercial garages with corrugated tin roofs. The property which is now Mayhew Lane was what resembled an abandoned field with tall wild grass and debris. What were the garages are now a group of resort shops and a parking lot. Continuing down Dock St, on the right, is a Chevrolet car garage, it extends to the water, assorted sheds and small buildings housing more working fisherman shacks and commercial enterprises. Then comes the Coal Wharf, with its large overhead walkway to move coal from barges to piles by type. The coal to be delivered to island homes for heating and cooking stoves.

Next comes a railway into the water to haul boats out to do maintenance on them. A large winch is at the head with cranks to be manned by 2 strong men to supply the power. This remains in use today. Then comes more fishermen shacks and finally the Town or Commercial Wharf with its large fishing vessels stacked alongside. In summer you could

Gem hauled out

buy lobster, sea scallops and fish right off the vessel that caught them. The Coal Wharf is now the Shanty Restaurant. What is now the Old Sculpin Art Gallery was then the workshop of Manuel S. Roberts, builder of Cat Boats. He was called the "Old Sculpin" thus the name of the Art Gallery. The Sculpin is a fish, but his friendly nick name was based more on his manner and perception. The Town Dock was very vital, My mother told me the ferry to New Bedford would arrive at night, and a traveler going to new Bedford the next day, could go aboard the night before an rent a state room. The next day you wake up in New Bedford. I would remember large commercial fishing boats stacked 2 or 3 deep if stormy weather was forecast.

It is a very key time for Edgartown too. The Town is starting to change from a small fishing village where a large population of immigrants from the Azores are making their way into the community. In the beginning they came from the Whaling industry. Whaling was a hard life, the voyages were long up to 3 to 4 years in some cases. Crews were hard to find. The Azores were located a first stop for ships heading out to Europe. Crews could be picked up there as the Islands were remote and work hard to find. The Prada's were part of that generation and Tony and his brothers and sisters as first generation, right at the start of dynamic changes. Tony's son in law would come from the Irish movement to Boston and Worcester.

The wife of another Portuguese immigrant, Manuel Mello, Maxi, who came over as a bride, is recorded by local historian as talking about her first

Very early views of the EYC and Inn to be from Osborn's Wharf.

Lower two buildings on Main St., are where the Annex will be built.

introduction to the others in similar circumstance to her husband. It was the day she met the 5 Manuels. Manuel was a very popular Portuguese name. My mother always joked you can ask any Portuguese family "How is your uncle Manuel and they will always acknowledge they have one".

Most were fishermen, working from 20 to 30-foot working catboats that were staked out in front of the Harborside Inn. I do not think the Prada's were whalers but Farmers and fishermen, who picked up on the migration to New Bedford and the Islands.

The Inn wing expands, each expansion adding new guest rooms and dining rooms, and the Annex appears for the first time.

7

1922

Tony and Jenny go on to expand the Inn itself, adding a large expansion onto the waterfront Side of the inn and interior. They continue accumulation of land on Main Street all the way down to the Harbor. In 1922 he files a plan of the land in the registry of deeds to install a stone bulkhead and pier. The Inn is starting to take shape, building a base, expanding operations consolidating as shown under the land plan of 1922.

With the new pier, Tony enlists his brother Frank into putting together a fleet of small sail boats for a summer rental fleet. These will line the new pier and be available to sail-your-self-rentals. Most of these will be smaller cat boats of 16 feet to 20 feet. Even more popular, retired older fishermen will be employed as captains to take families and individuals on harbor tours or teach summer visitors how to sail. This will continue to be a very popular enterprise all the way into the 1970's. The boats will be hauled each fall and put in again each spring. The hurricanes will challenge this concept, but it is just too good a business. They build a new boat house to use as an operation base. As a kid growing up it was great fun to sit in on the old timers who sat around in rocking chairs waiting for customers to take out for a sail. These old guys told long tales of fishing and adventures all over the globe. If only a recording machine had been available.

Capt's Rose, F.Prada, Fisher, C. Muldaur, D. Brantigan

HSI Maids 1926

The Convery's

Irene Louise Prada
1929

Leo & Irene, 1927

Jane & Tony Prada   April 29 '29.   Leo & Irene Convery

EDGARTOWN GIRL TO WED APRIL 29

EDGARTOWN, April 18 (Special)—Miss Irene L. Prada, daughter of Mr. and Mrs. Antone Prada, owners of the Harborside Inn here, will marry Leo J. Convery, at the St. Andrews Episcopal church here at noon on April 29. The wedding will be held at the church with the rector, Rev. Mr. Patineau, officiating.

The couple are planning to make their home here and this summer they will manage the Harborside Inn. They filed their marriage intentions in Worcester today, where Miss Prada is a hostess at the Georgian cafeteria. The bride will wear her mother's wedding dress at the ceremony and her friend, Miss Eleanor Phelps, of New York, will be bridesmaid. Miss Prada is a graduate of the Northfield seminary and the Y. W. C. A. school of domestic science in Boston. Mr. Convery is a shipping clerk for the Wilson Co. in Worcester.

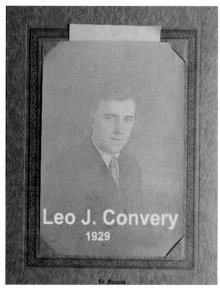

Leo J. Convery
1929

The Inn continues to thrive and grow into the late 20's. it is great time for the family in 1929, Leo J. Convery marries Irene Louise Prada, April 29, 1929, Big things are afoot. Their wedding announcement states that they will be the new innkeepers after their marriage.

Little did they know that on October 24, 1929, would be the start of the great Depression, with all that goes with it. Living through it took all the stamina one could muster to make ends meet. 1929 to 1933, will prove to be terrible years for the country and the world and especially for the Converys, they will struggle to make it.

1930- 1939

Tragedy Strikes in 1930, Tony Prada at age 52 goes into the hospital for a tonsillitis operation and dies of complications. Newley weds Leo and Irene find themselves in the

Inn business. They will become the driving forces that build this into the Islands only waterfront inn and a premier resort. The Main Inn building in its early configurations had about 8 to 10 rooms. Before long the Inn will grow to have over 100 rooms in multiple Edgartown Captains homes on South Water St and along Main Street.

Leo J. Convery came from a family of 9 kids, he was the oldest, had gone to work early after his father left the family. He went to work to support his mother and the 8 brothers and sisters. He would go on to be able to buy their home in Worcester and hire some of them to work at the Inn.

Work was for him a natural thing. I came along in 1933. I must have been at least 5 or 6. Years old before I had any real recollections. I very much remember his work routine. He would rise every morning a 5 am and go over to the office. He told me he got a day's work done by the time everyone else showed up. Making a go of the Inn was just going to be a lot of hard work but he was prepared to do it and he would do it. My wanting to sleep in when coming back from school off the Vineyard, really bothered him. I was urged to rise at 6 am so I would have longer to "loaf"! Inactivity in his son was not something he was willing to endure. I had to go to work early, washing dishes, polishing brass fireplace fittings, sweeping sidewalks and the like, Later in my early teens, my friends got wise and called me to join them. Stopping by meant running into my dad. Spotting 2 or more idle boys, my father always had some furniture to move.

After the Convery's took over the Inn operation, it became a point of making the Inn over to suit their idea of what and how an inn should operate, rooms had to be refurbished, repainted, and changed, closets added, bathrooms installed where none were before.

The 30's proved to be growing pains with the Inn and its operations being consolidated with good staff and a following of customers. The Inn operated from June 15 to Labor Day, a very short season. Over the winter, other work had to be done to make it through.

Tony's, wife Jenny or grandma as I would call her, continued to live in the former EYC building now called the Prada House up until her death in 1946. As I look back and try to remember her, she was a very active lady, and thrifty. My father and mother were a bit afraid of her as she still had some control over the Inn, but for me she made the best stuffed raisin cookies and lemon meringue pie. I regret I never got her recipes for either.

One of the big purchases for the Converys in 1932 was the home directly across the street from the Inn as a home for themselves and their growing family. My sister Nancy was born in 1931. My Mom would rule the Inn and home with frequent trips across South Water St.

The Annex was the first outbuilding to be added on to the Inn. It is hard from the photos to determine exactly when it built. It shows up in photos between 1937 and 1939. The Annex sits between Main St and the Inn Grounds on the site of the Munroe and John Bent Properties on Main Street. It is a two-story wood frame building, and has 3 rooms on the Inn's gardens, two retail stores on Main Street and 8 rooms above.

This is a first hint that the inn is becoming more than a rooming house and tourism is making a market in Edgartown. Leo Convery ran a liquor store out of one of the Main St. Stores in this building. Receiving the license after liquor became legal again. He would Move it across to a Main Street store he would acquire in the 1939 or 1940. The Harborside Liquor Store would become the go to store in Edgartown for fine wines and liquors. It was a year-round business.

The Convery's are out to make a difference on the Inn's operation. They change the Inn's dining over to the American Plan which will include meals. This sets the Inns room rates to include 3 meals a day. When you book the room, you get to dine in the hotel for breakfast, lunch, and dinner, it's a better deal for the Innkeeper and probably for the guest as well as there are not a lot of fine dining places in the town.

1938

The '38 hurricane rips up the town, this is a major storm still noted for its ferocity. The hurricane of 1938 is one of my first real memories. We lived directly across the street from the Inn's front door. It is secure but, the Inn is so vulnerable. I can understand only later what must be going through my father's mind and how he dealt with the devastation he was seeing the next day. I knew the hurricane struck after dark and midnight was the worst. The pictures of the 1944 Hurricane will show similar scenarios, that will illustrate the aftershock.

Seeing my Father and other men going in and out our front door and hearing the raging winds outside. I could sense their concerns. The morning after was frightening on seeing the disaster at a 5-year-olds level.

Getting through this set back seemed to only motivate new courses of action.

1939

This is the year that they acquire what is the Captain Ripley house, a very impressive 3 story building with grounds from the South Water Street to the harbor and a wood pier out into the Harbor. This leaves the Harbor Club between the Inn and the Ripley house as ripe for the plucking.

The depression is said to end about this time. The world is still unstable and the threat of war in Europe is churning away. The island is growing but things are stabilizing on the home front.

1940 to 1945

The 40's would turn out to be extremely influential on the development of the Inn. The war, hurricanes, and post war changes to the economy will bring big changes to the town.

The Harbor Club will be acquired just as the war begins in 1942. This is the building and land to the immediate west edge of the Inn land, all the way to the harbor. The Home Club is shown in post cards with the large wood pier into the harbor. It is between the Captain Ripley house acquired in 1939 and completes a large expansion of the Inn up South Water Street.

SOUTH WATER STREET, EDGARTOWN, MASS. **1920**

South Water Street, near Main Street   Edgartown, Mass.   **1920**

The Sign embossed into the glass of the front door says "Chappaquiddick House. This was the Edgartown home of John Jeremiah, who owned a large waterfront home on Chappy, and used this for an intown home base. It is immediately leased out to the Navy as the Officers Club for the command staff at the new Navy training facility at what will become the islands main airport.

The Inns operation takes on a new dimension as the war takes over the world and the Island. Blackouts require no lights to be shown at night and Leo Convery becomes an air raid warden, with duties to patrol the street and look for light leaking out from black out curtains people had to install.

Food becomes a problem, rationing begins. if a guest can still come to the island, they must be fed. Getting food is now an issue. Guests must bring their own ration books. Fortunately, there is a large turkey farm on the Vineyard. The buyer of Turkeys must supply the labor to kill and dress the turkeys. Picking pin feathers has now become my position at 10 years old. The Turkeys are hung by their feet to an overhead conveyer, killed by electrocution and then are dragged over a big 3- or 4-foot-wide spinning drum with flexible rubber 2-inch-wide finger like stubs all over it to remove most of the feathers. Then the naked turkey gets to me and a few others to remove what the drum missed, called pin feathers because a lot of them are just the broken off feathers.

The turkeys were raised in a big field in Vineyard Haven, along the road from Edgartown. The farm today is now occupied by the senior living facility "Haven Side" and I think "Carroll's Trucking". This was Burke's Turkey Farm where Turkeys were made to roost on a series of log rail fences, 4 ft off the ground, visible from the highway and lighted at night. The rails spelled out "BURKES". The farm was owned by the owner of Sweetheart Soap we were told.

Turkeys and fish are now the base of the Inn's dinners. Turkey was served many varied and multiple ways. The chef at that time was John king. John king was deaf, and every order had to be written down. With the dining room being on the floor level above the kitchen, this was necessary any way. He was Chef for the Inn for several years coming over to work each summer from his home in Wareham. Being deaf he was obviously exempt from the draft.

Each summer he stayed in a room, in a building the Inn maintained for staff all summer. As I recall during the war years the staff were mostly women, or older men. My uncle Bob who handled all the Inn's maintenance was off to China, serving as a plane maintenance specialist with General Chennault and the Flying Tigers.

The Dining Room

The dining room was in the back of the main building, on the street level floor, overlooking the harbor in the new wing of the hotel. It seated about 50 people and was served from a service room between the street and the dining room. This was where coffee was made, and initial salads and appetizers were put together. The baker worked from here to making bread and pastries, pies and cakes. Waiters and waitresses worked out of here.

The kitchen was below. The two functioned as follows:

There were two small service elevators, referred to as "dumb waiters", on the side of the service room, with a small chute about 3 by 4 inches between the dumb waiters. Each dumb waiter was about 3.5 ft. high, by 2 ft wide and 18 inches deep, that went to the kitchen below. They worked by a rope pully that spun a wheel above when the rope on the right was pulled it raised them, and the rope on the left, lowered them.

The waitresses would write the food order at the tables then take it to the "Dumb Waiters" and grab a metal clip on. This was clipped to the paper order slip to weight it down so it would not get stuck in the small chute. Then it is dropped in. She then pushes a button on the wall above, that sounds an alarm below. This will notify the attendant, in the kitchen below, that an order has been sent down. The attendant grabs the order, brings it over to the Chef's station for execution. When the order is ready, the attendant take the plates from the chef's work bench, over to the dumb waiter, puts it in. Then the attendant grabs the hoist rope and pulls it to take the hot foot up to the second level. He Pushes the alarm button. The attendant in the above service room, removes it from the dumbwaiter and gives it to the waitress to bring out to her customers.

A baker worked in the service level, but all other kitchen staff were below. All dishes were washed below, so all went up and down on the two dumb waiters, hand hoisted each time.

All the waiters and waitress and other staff were housed in buildings owned by the Inn. Boys Dorms and Girls Dorms. Uniforms were worn by most of the service staff and given out by the housekeeper. The wait staff maintained their own uniforms.

Wait and kitchen staff were fed three meal a day, from a room off the kitchen below. There was a lot of camaraderie among the staff and good friendly kidding and joking.

There was one large walk in refrigerator in the main kitchen. Reserve food was kept in cold storage in Lambert's Cove, in a conversion of an old icehouse into new facility out on the shore of "Icehouse Pond". This was used only a few years back by actually cutting ice in winter from the pond and storing it in the "Icehouse" through the year providing cold storage. It had now been converted to mechanical freezing machines that operated on ammonia. A lot of food shipped in now was stored here, bought when it was available, processed and then frozen to be used later. I remember going up there with my uncle to retrieve food for the kitchen. The smell of ammonia was bad but the cold unbearable. It was a balmy 75 to 80 in the summer heat outside and 35 inside, for a 12-year-old not a fun time.

The war years 1942 to 1946- Edgartown

The Navy came in and built an airport on a large part of the State Forest. This was purposed to training Navy pilots to fly and to bomb and strafe. Noman's island was turned into a target area too. Along with the base at the airfield, a practice bombing facility was built at South Beach. This involved building a large circle measuring about a half a mile across with a large sand-berm built around edge. Targets were established in the center. Fighter planes would stack up over the Town, 12 to 20 at a time and dive bomb and strafe the targets at Katama. At nighttime they would come again and bomb with practice bombs on Cape Pogue Pond using parachute flares to light up the target. Edgartown was a very active participant in more than training from the airport. The harbor and South Beach were being used to train troops for the invasion of Normandy. From the waterfront we would see streams of landing barges full of troops steam by Chappy Point through the harbor to a destination at Katama. We kids would row out to greet them as they motored through. There were no houses at that time at Katama of any significance. The troops would camp out up there. This was a magnet to kids in town. We would venture out hoping to come back with loot in the form of k rations or canteens and such. When the troops had liberty, Lots of soldiers would be on the streets, especially at the liquor stores and the USO. When they left town, there was often a line of beer bottles on Main Street. Kids got out early the next morning collecting them for the nickel back.

1944 Hurricane

The hurricane of 1944 was a major event for the Town and especially for the Inn. A very intense storm and very destructive of both the ships that were torn from their moorings and blown in to wreak havoc on the docks and waterfront buildings. Much like the 1938 storm, the Inn's fleet of rental boats were very much a part of that as the photos will show. This on top of a war going on and all the hardships, staying in business was not easy.

Photos show the carnage wrought on the Inn, with boats stacked like cord wood on one another. An interesting boat of note, that came ashore by the Coal Wharf, and the Yacht Club, off Dock Street was the Manxman. A prewar yacht, the largest yawl rig in the world at 102 feet. She had been captained by a local, Captain Sam Norton. He was known for bringing it in under full sail, tacking off the Yacht Club pier, then tacking again to bring it up harbor to its mooring. The Manxman had been mothballed with all rigging removed and a wood cover built over it for the duration of the war. Blown ashore, it wrecked a few fishing boats but, lived to sail again.

From Osbornes Warf 1944

1944

The Manxman in 1944 and after 1945 to 1949

Part of the restoration of the main building and dining room occurred in the period between the 1945 and 1949. The dining room was moved to the lower garden level by building out from the existing wing toward the Home Club, now the Chappy House. A large deck would go on top and full windows on the new room below, would give it a great garden and harbor View. A large grand staircase was built to take diners to and from the old dining room which was made over into a card room and sitting room.

The last Captain's Home, the Milton House, with the great Pagoda Tree out front was acquired in 1945. The imposing Pagoda Tree out front was a great acquisition, my father will hold it in a special place and its care is assured as long as he will live. The tree was brought to the Island by Captain Thomas Milton on his whaling ship in a flowerpot and planted when he built his home here. The contract to build the home was hung in the front hall for years, Specifying so many carts of lumber. These 3 homes will be used pretty much as they are inside for a few years as rental rooms by the Inn.

An interesting note, Jimmy Cagney the movie actor would buy the next home up the street on the other side of the Pagoda Tree. Jimmy had a farm up in Chilmark, where he could hide out from an adoring public, but he had adopted two children and wanted them to be in a more active environment of Edgartown. There is a post card showing my father talking to two kids under the Pagoda Tree. I think these are the Cagney kids. They were about the same age as my two younger sister and the Cagney kids hung out a bit with them.

Slowly these grand Captain's homes will get bathrooms added in and eventually a full make over. This acquisition completes the full circuit of land from Osborn's Wharf, up Main St and along south Water Street. The street front along that side of South Water Street will stay the same from the 20's up to the present.

What most people today do not realize about these fine waterfront Captain's homes, is that the harbor view was not important to the owners. The fine sitting rooms and bedrooms faced the street. The Harbor was where they earned their living, it was smelly. The ladies wanted to see who was going by in the new carriage, The maid's rooms, scullery, and kitchens were on the back or water side. You see this in the photos. The Ripley House's third floor was a series of small maid's rooms. The bathrooms were down the hall. My father had small sinks installed in the rooms. I remember these being rented out for weekly or even monthly to single elderly ladies for longer periods. Their "steamer Trunks", so called, would arrive by Express trucks, and dropped off in front of the Inn. Sometimes it was my job to help wrestle them to the third-floor bedroom, where they took up a great deal of the room' space.

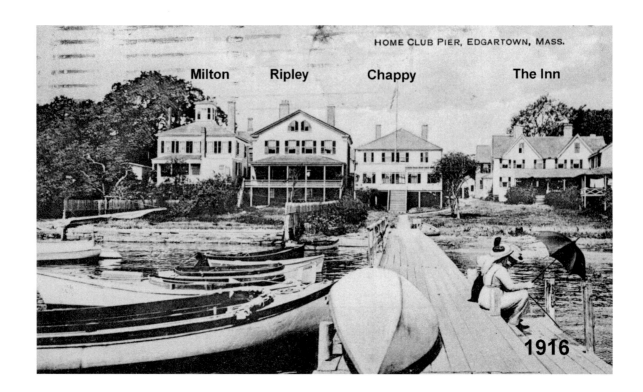

Milton   Ripley   Chappy   The Inn

1916

1947

My uncle had returned from his adventures in China with the Flying Tigers and my father thought he should be involved in more of the business. The 1944 hurricane had demolished the small cottage at the foot of the former EYC building still referred to as the Prada house. This was a prime site, and it was decided to make it into a cocktail bar and small restaurant. It became the "Boat House Bar & Grill". Serving an informal Menu and with a dance floor and a raised musician platform. The building was a one story rounded roof structure. Ostensibly a covered deck was built around the core bar room, dance floor, all with a nautical theme showing off some of my father's collections of marine antiques. It became instantly popular with the guests and the town.

The hotel guests with the American Plan, having all their meals at the Inn, would come to the Boathouse Bar for a cocktail starting at 5 to 5:30 pm. Have drinks and a dance then venture to the Inn for dinner. A first seating at 6:00 pm and the second seating at 8:00 pm. The most memorable band to me was the Zarde Trio, Two Brothers, Sam was the leader with an accordion, his brother played the bass and a piano Player. Great dance music, They lasted into the 50's. We had a series of great musicians after them, like Carlos Piantini, the first violinist of the New York Philharmonic for the summer. Leonard Bernstein, the director, would sometimes drop in and accompany him. There was also a memorable bartender from Florida who would come back every year for at least 10 years. His name was Xavier. A small wiry built man. According to our guests, his martinis were the best ever. He never got overwhelmed no matter how busy it got. Very proud of his work. The Boathouse would last up until the 60's when it was torn down to build the Navigator restaurant.

1948

A new chef arrives, Sam Pappus, a Greek, and a Patriarch of a large family. He is a Chef at Harvard University, so our short summer season in Edgartown fits his schedule. I work in the kitchen in the summers, at least 4 of the Pappus family are named George, so with the other workers we all become George. There is a lot of camaraderie in the kitchen staff too. We serve 3 meals a day, breakfast from 8 am to 9:30, lunch from noon to 2:00 pm, and dinner from 6:00 pm to 8:00. This means the waitress and waiter staff work all three meals but have a few hours off between them. Time to go to the beach or off to a movie at night. Guests in the dining room are assigned a specific table for their stay and the same waiter or waitress so a relationship can be established, and a good tip will result.

Each Summer season, I work a different station, starting in the bake shop a helper to the baker. The baker an older man, is a very talented baker. He makes the best brioche, his dough takes a week to develop, pulling it out each day to add butter and turn to build layers. I get to bake pies, and taking a fresh apple or blueberry pie out hot and steaming from the oven was great. While new at the job, I got to cut a slice to devour, it is tasty, but the thrill wears off after a month, it is not the treat it was in the beginning. We have a problem, one evening, there is a convention in the hotel of 60. We have prepared 60 individual baked Alaska's, which is a layer of cake with ice cream in a small deep bowl with a meringue top. We cannot get the top to brown in the oven. The head maintenance person Gene Belisle goes by and said he can help. He bring in his plumbing torch and browns the tops in minutes and saves the day!

I move on to other stations each year, from the Garde d 'Mange, building salads, making dressing, working the front desk, learning to fix most anything that needs fixing. The sailboat fleet is always in need of repair or hauling in for the winter or putting out for the summer. The fleet is great for time off too. The work is challenging, and I build a resume for entry to the Cornell Hotel School in fall of 1952. I put in 4 years here, graduating in 1956.

Harborside Inn Fleet and Skipper   Edgartown, Mass.   Island of Martha's Vineyard

1949

The Islands tourist season was stretching out now what used to be the Season from June 15 to Labor day, has now grown to encompass June and September.

The Bass and Bluefish Derby was created by the MV Chamber of Commerce to bring in fall business. Leo J Convery was a founder of the Chamber and served as a director up to the 70's. The Derby is still going strong today in 2023.

This same year, 1949, the Prada House, the old former EYC building, gets torn down and rebuilt, rounding out the inn's grounds with a new up to date building. Two new shops for Main Street and 4 rooms on the garden and 8 above very similar to the Annex. Built in the early 30's.

The Lure of Edgartown, Mass.

1941

1950's

The 1950's will bring a lot of rapid changes to the Inn, new buildings, a pool, big change to the 3 captains homes, completion of the Prada House, and dealing with 2 hurricanes.

1950 brings a new home into the Inns group. This home across is across South Water street beside the Family home owned by Errol Fisher. This would be converted into rooms and named the Fisher House. Not fancy rooms but for Edgartown, affordable. The Inn has become very popular, and the rooms were non-waterfront, in an affordable category and most anything could be rented in high season. It includes a garage building in the back with a room over it. This back building will become the center for a new Gardener, John Perkins. A small green house will be constructed between the family home and the Fisher house. Gardner John will develop the Inns gardens from here into a spectacular category. The Begonias he plants on the walk down into the garden from South Water St. between the Chappy house and the Main Building will be noted by all as very special. John will also gather seeds from the Pagoda tree and bring two new Pagoda trees into life. The first is planted in front of the Ripley house but become too big blocking the view. It is dug up and donated to the former Edgartown Library, now the Carnegie building on North Water St. and the other donated to the MV Museum property on School and Cook St. Now operated as the historic Norton Home as the museum has moved out of town.

New pool and building's water fronts   1958

1958

1952

1952 The Jeremiah building will be built on the lower lawn of the Milton house. There was no zoning in Edgartown and no building inspector. My father called me one morning and said let go down and stake out where we want to build this building. We did, then called Harold Dugan a builder we have used since I was in the picture, he sent his foreman down the next day and staked out the actual building. Construction of the foundation began that week and the building was completed several months later.

1953 A swimming pool would be added to the center of the gardens which would serve to pull the whole inn together as one unit.

The gardens would get made over with a swimming pool and deck filled with lounge chairs and served by a pool attendant.

A sea wall would be built to hold the waterfront and tie the whole. Properties together

1953 is special for me. Among the new batch of waitresses is my wife to be. Each year our summer staff come from the young college students. This year is no different but very different. We establish a relationship, so she will return the next year in 1954. As a family working at running the Inn, we meet every morning at a family table for breakfast, to exchange information and get our orders. My father who is somewhat demanding and has a short fuse at times, got upset over some infraction our cute waitress has made and makes a statement that she should be fired. I have to inform him "Dad", "You cannot fire that girl!" As I am going to marry her! Which I did in 1956 after graduating from Cornell. Alison and I now have 67 great years of marriage together.

These next years would also be very involved in major change to the total Inn's composition and over all buildings to unite it into a whole operating Resort in the middle of Edgartown, taking advantage of its location directly on the harbor.

Harborside Inn
EDGARTOWN, MASSACHUSETTS

Date_____

Please send me further information as to available accommodations. My party will consist of...............persons.

We will require...........doubles and/or...........singles.

The dates of our HOLIDAY will be

.............................to...........................

We would like the rate to be.............................

NAME_____

STREET_____

CITY_____STATE_____

For a definite reservation please enclose a deposit of $25 per person.

We will acknowledge by return mail.

NO PETS PLEASE · **FREE PARKING**

ROOM RATES — 1956

JULY 1 - SEPT. 1

TWIN BEDROOMS/Private Bath ....$28-$32

TWIN BEDROOMS
Private Bath, Garden Side ....$32-$36

TWIN BEDROOMS
Private Bath, Garden Side with Balcony......$36-$40

SINGLE with BATH $16-$18
SINGLE with RUNNING WATER $16

JUNE 21 - JULY 1
SEPT. 1 - SEPT. 8

TWIN BEDROOMS/Private Bath ....$24-$28

TWIN BEDROOMS
Private Bath, Garden Side ....$28-$32

TWIN BEDROOMS
Private Bath, Garden Side with Balcony ....$32-$36

SINGLE with BATH $14-$16
SINGLE with RUNNING WATER $14

Rate depends upon location and size of room and is quoted daily and American Plan (with meals).

For Reservations write or phone

Harborside Inn
Edgartown 415

Martha's Vineyard Island, Mass.

1951

Waterfront Scene, Edgartown, Mass.

0C604-N

27

1954

Two hurricanes arrive, Carol and Edna in 1954, within weeks apart. Both were category 3 storms. Carol arrives in August 25, but it hits way down the Coast in Connecticut. For the island, this saves us from a lot of destruction. We got hit with high water and some wind. Carol would be most destructive in Ct. The storm was declared so destructive, its name was retired from use naming storms in the future. Hurricane Edna would bring a very different outcome for Edgartown and the Inn. The Eye of the storm would pass right over us on September 11. The Inn is occupied with guests. The Inn's food is served from the lower garden level dining room and serviced by the kitchen on the same level. Wind was clocked at 75 to 95 MPH with higher gusts. We take guests out of the Jeremiah house in the morning by rowboat. The wind is blowing full gale and more, the water is rising up over the grounds and into the dining room all the way up into the Kitchen. Food service is suspended for the next two days. I haul a few of the catboats drifting into the grounds, out to the Osborn parking lot walking waist deep in water and tie them to the telephone pole there. Other boats come in drift up into the gardens and pile up against the Inn. To illustrate how high the water becomes, the Cat Boats in the harbor in front of the inn are tied onto and old car tire the floats around a wood piling or stake that is driven into the harbor bottom and sticks up 6 to 7 ft above high tide. The boats become free when the tire floats up over the top of the pole on rising water. All the staff pitch in the next day to restore the damage, move the boats back to the harbor, and clean out the dining room and kitchen which were inundated. The wood floors in the Jeremiah house, holds water so we have to drill holes to let the water drain out. It is all done with old fashioned hand twist augers as the electricity is off over most of the island. It will take days to restore service.

1956

1956 is another memorable year especially for me. I graduate from Cornell in May and marry Alison McFarlin, former summer waitress Scottish name as my grandfather did with Jenny Hoey from Glasgow

1957

It is hard to pin down the exact year that the three Captains houses got a full renovation, they do not show on pictures in 1954 and they do show in 1958, so they probably got made over in 1956 and 57. The construction cut off the back half of each building with all the smaller rooms and rebuilt with 3 room across the back with three stories to each, and a sitting deck on each waterfront room, new baths. This left the street side as they were built, a sensitive use of the historic past of the buildings.

With the Prada house replacement and the makeover of the 3 Captain's homes the Inn is pretty much developed as it is today. The time-share make over will be the next big makeover of the interiors and exteriors in 80's.

The Next big undertaking for the Convery family would not happen until 1964, the new Navigator Restaurant and Boat house Bar

BOATHOUSE BAR, HARBORSIDE INN, EDGARTOWN 1960'S

1954

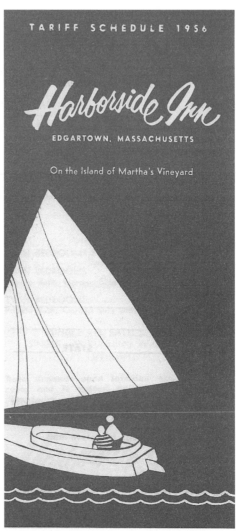

MIAMI BEACH, FLA.

"Spectra-Color"
POSTCARD

TV, Radio, Comics
Features, Weather

The Even

Worcester, Mass.

Leo J. Convery stands in front of his Harborside Inn, Edgartown, where he employs more than 100 persons. In 1929, he employed two.

Innkeeper on Island for 33 Years
Former City Man Operates 100-Room Vineyard Hostelry

By NANCY LOWE GRAY

EDGARTOWN — A former Worcester man has become one of the biggest taxpayers on this island since he came here in 1929 to operate a modest 18-room inn. Today, Leo J. Convery owns the Harborside Inn, which features 100 rooms with private baths, plus 40 housekeeping units, along with a spacious motel. A fleet of 30 pleasure crafts are moored at the private piers in front of his rambling, waterfront inn.

Other Convery enterprises dot the quaint 30-mile island with its eight towns. The husky, congenial innkeeper is president of Edgartown Chamber of Commerce and is a member of the board of trustees at Martha's Vineyard Hospital.

the lobbies, restaurant and boathouse bar. Ships' lanterns, harpoons, ropes and chip models of the famous whalers that once sailed the seven seas are eye-catchers.

Today the Convery enterprises are run by the entire family.

The Converys have four children and seven grandchildren. They are Mrs. Arthur W. Young, who manages the Carol Apartments here for her father; Mrs. David M. Brown of Haddonfield, N.J.; Margery P. Convery, a sophomore at Colby, now studying at Harvard Summer School, and Leo Prada Convery, a graduate of Cornell University's hotel school. Young Convery manages the inn, along with his brother-in-law, Arthur W. Young.

He has three sisters, Mrs. Carlton Gray of East Princeton, Mrs. Thomas J. Lane of 44 Blossom St., and Mrs. Beatrice Kanaley of 11 Berkshire St.; two brothers, Gerald Convery of 50 Greenhill Pkwy. and Edward F. Convery of 21 Home St., and an uncle, Arthur Labrie of 11 Berkshire St.

Another brother, Robert E. Convery, is associated with Leo here.

City Council Sets Schedule For Summer

The City Council is now on its summer schedule with its

New C To Los

The future of a new city church appears to ardy.

Founded Dec. 31, 1961 S. Paul Carlyss, Calvar was intended to be an " tic center," revivalist believing in the literal the Bible.

Calvary Temple, which church at 16 Greenv owned (and formerly occ Emanuel Lutheran Chu lose its pastor when Mrs. Carlyss leave A White Plains, N.Y. Mrs will become director of the public school system

Pastor 3 Year

Rev. Mr. Carlyss, a Sweden, was pastor of sembly of God, 635 Grove years before forming church. He has served cl Joliet, Ill.; Colorado Spri Minneapolis, Minn.; Chic Pasadena, Calif.; Arcad and New York City.

Rev. Mr. Carlyss said I believed that the South England District, Asser God, would buy the prop install Rev. Woodrow present pastor of the L Assembly of God Church tor of Calvary Temple.

Resignation Refus

However, when Rev. cher submitted his resig the Leominster church, bers refused to accept him to stay on another agreed, thus disqualifyin for the Worcester pastora

Rev. George Flower, di perintendent of Assemblie said that the district's purchase the property him Rev. Mr. Fletcher's avail

"We don't have any int of taking it over." he s

Worcester Mass newspaper

The Navigator Restaurant 1964-1965

Navigator Restaurant under construction April 1964

Staffing was always a full-time job. 40's to 60's

Over the years a myriad of staff would circulate through the various jobs. The head house keepers and room maids, parlor maids, kitchen staff, head chef and line cooks, bakers, kitchen workers, salad workers, coffee makers night cleaners, pot cleaners, dish washers, front desk clerks, Telephone operators, bell hops, back-office staff, reservations managers, bookkeeper, night bookkeeper auditor, night watchman, grounds keepers, head gardener, maintenance manager, assistant, boat rental fleet manager/captain and staff, Boathouse Bar manager, helpers, waiters, cooks, bartenders, musicians and more. It was and is a full-time job keeping the Inn running and fully staffed, generally the department heads would hire their own staffs.

For the 40's and part of the 50's whole groups of staff would come from the Florida Resorts. They operated in the winter but not in the summers, and the cooking schools, such as the Culinary Institute and Johnson Wales for the kitchen who need to work for their summer off period. They also liked our short season. Ealy season were from Mid-June to the week after Labor Day. Our season was so short, many of the Florida workers left us in Sept after we closed to work in New Hampshire and Vermont, with a longer season. Then they would head back to Florida.

Many of the Staff would return year after year and it was like home coming for them and my parents. Eventually the Inn was able to house all the staff in Inn owned housing around the town. A good percentage were islanders.

1963- 1980

This would be a big step for the Inn, it would mark the end of the American Plan, with the full 3 meals a day priced into and included in the room rate. This is called the European plan. The New restaurant will serve breakfast, lunch, and dinner. A new team of chefs and cooks from the CIA (Culinary Institute of America) would staff the kitchen.

The Boat house bar so popular over the years, gets torn down and a new building take its place. The search for a builder brings Stanley Snyder to the Island. He goes on to develop condominiums at South Beach and his son develops a hotel, the Winnitu, out of the bones of the former Katama Shores Condominium which was part of the old Navy Operations Facility. The new restaurant building is panelized and goes up quickly. It quickly becomes a landmark waterfront restaurant. A full-service restaurant is on the top floor and a partial replica of the Boathouse Bar on the first floor with a dance band and seating inside and outside in a waterfront patio.

The Harborside Inn continues to operate under the Convery Sr's. direction until 1970 When my sister and brother-in-law and I lease it as partners. Leo J, Convery and Irene P. Convery were killed in a car accident in Erie P. in 1978. My partners and I decided to time share the hotel 1980 and it was completed by 1985.

In Memoriam

Irene Louise Convery   Leo John Convery

TEN

VINEYARD GAZETTE

Martha's Vineyard's Newspaper for 130 Years

Established 1846 — A Non-Political Journal of Island Life

Edgartown, Martha's Vineyard, Mass. 02539

Elizabeth Bowie Hough and Henry Beetle Hough
Publishers 1920 — 1965

•

Henry Beetle Hough, *Editor*

•

Sally Fulton Reston and James Reston, *Publishers*

•

Richard Reston, *General Manager*

•

Douglas Cabral, *Managing Editor*
William A. Caldwell, *Associate Editor*

A Deep Impress Upon the Times

What the history of Edgartown would have been in the transition years from 1930 to 1976 without the influence of Mr. and Mrs. Leo J. Convery is impossible to imagine. They took over the Harborside Inn not only at the outset of the great depression but at a time when old customs and patterns of vacation living were being revolutionized by the new mobility of the automobile and other basic structures in modern life. Many a rambling hotel structure on a New England hilltop or headland would soon become an empty relic, memorial to times forgotten. With the Harborside it was different.

The Converys, in planning imaginatively for the future, brought change to the Vineyard, but more than that they shaped the new times to an Island adaptation which softened and harmonized the unavoidable confrontation. In long perspective the impact of their evolving enterprise on the Island economy and summer mode seems important enough to be called decisive.

They took over the Harborside when it consisted of the single historic building that Mrs. Convery's father had acquired in 1914, later restoring it, and establishing the boat yard at the harbor front. A major addition was that of the large building on lower Main street in 1936. The whaling captains' houses of South Water street, still bearing the names of the owners, were added — as it now seems — almost year by year, and their identities on the street side were kept unaltered, retaining the Edgartown tradition. Neither the depression nor the lean war years prevented the growth of the Harborside with a physical presence now taken for granted.

All this would not have been possible without the personal qualities of Mr. and Mrs. Convery, and it is their warmth and cordiality that will remain alive and meaningful as much as or more than the structures they built. The news of their accidental deaths in Pennsylvania can be described as shattering, and their absence in all sorts of Vineyard relationships will be felt in a long future.

Other Convery Businesses.

All while the development of the Harborside Inn is going on, the Converys would develop what was known as the Corner Market Building, occupied by their Harborside Liquor Store, on the corner of Main St. and North Water St. with offices on the second floor and other stores on lower Main Street.

They built a new business out of the old School House, and new construction of what would become the Carol Apartments on Pease's Point Way and Mill Street in Edgartown starting in the 40's and is now a condominium operation called Edgartown, Commons.

He was ½ owner of the Boston House, a restaurant on the Main Street of Oak Bluffs.

In the 40' to 60's he owned and operated a restaurant called the Georgian Cafeteria in Springfield Mass.

He owned the Old Village Inn and 10 room Inn in Oak Bluffs Eastville area. It was sold to the Hospital for Expansion,

He owned the former Mary Guerin Inn at Eastville Beach by the Bridge between Oak Bluffs and Vineyard Haven.

On their deaths in 1978 the property which became Eastville Beach, was given to conservation in their memory by their 4 Children.

Leo J Convery & Leo P Convery family

This has been an adventure in setting out our family history and recording the building of an Island resort Inn by and island family. If there are any errors in dates or other information, they are my fault as my memory bank at my age, has too much information. To be able to retrieve anything at all accurately is a special occasion.

Leo P. Convery March 2023

A timeline of
Harborside Inn property acquisition

Tony Prada buys:

The Inn	Bought	1914
The EYC (Prada house)	Bought	1922
John Bent Main St (Annex Land)	Bought	1925
The Convery's take over	Innkeepers	1930
Annex building	Built	1933-1935
Capt. Ripley House	Bought	1939
Chappaquiddick house	Bought	1942
Capt. Thomas Milton House	Bought	1945
Capt. Jeremiah House built	Built	1954 -1956
Parking lot	Bought and built	1953
3 Captains Homes	Re-built	1954-1955
Pool	Built	1954-1955
Time Shared Inn		1980 -1985

Printed in the United States
by Baker & Taylor Publisher Services